Classic
Cottages

Classic Cottages

Cindy Smith Cooper

PRESS

Hoffman Media
1900 International Park Drive, Suite 50
Birmingham, Alabama 35243
hoffmanmedia.com

ISBN # 978-1-940772-50-9
Printed in China

83
PRESS

CONTENTS

Introduction

ottage style knows no boundaries. It lives in our dreams and imaginations in a host of romantic interpretations. For some, it might be an airy, light-filled farmhouse in the South of France or a quaint thatched-roof getaway tucked along the coast of Wales. Yet for others, it could mean the beautiful simplicity of a breezy saltbox bungalow by the sea or a humble one-room lake cabin nestled deep in the woods. Whatever your own personal vision, today's cottage style remains a composite of blissful imagery that is warmly inviting, utterly welcoming, and brimming with unpretentious, personable charm. In a sense, cottage style has always seemed to capture the truest essence of hearth and home.

Our own interpretations aside, key elements of traditional cottage style certainly still live at the core of its modern transformation. The word "cottage" itself continues to evoke images of modestly proportioned dwellings situated in rural or remote settings, with interiors generally consisting of small ground-floor living spaces containing cozy and often irregularly shaped rooms and one or two upper-floor bedrooms wedged up under the eaves.

Classic architectural features call to mind steeply pitched roofs with gables or clipped gables, flared eaves, a central dormer, thick porch posts, simplified Doric columns, tall and narrow multilight diamond-paned windows, arched doorways with decorative hardware, and oversize chimneys with decorative brick or stonework. Throughout history, we've romanticized these cottage dwellings as holiday homes, intimate getaways, and vacation refuges in which to escape from the stresses of everyday life.

While we continue to celebrate the beloved cottage style of the past, its widespread popularity has brought about a joyful evolution of the term—one that now embraces a much broader and more contemporary worldwide aesthetic. Today, we can delight in whimsical examples of this genre most anywhere and everywhere, from rambling country farmhouses and roomy metropolitan lofts to charming urban bungalows and tiny inner-city flats.

Borrowing from diverse historic influences, including 18th-century English cottage, traditional French country, and 20th-century shabby chic, modern cottage style embodies a beautiful blend of the old and the new, the rustic and the refined, the classic and the contemporary. Today's cottage style is fresh and versatile—no rules apply. It lets us mix patterns with lighthearted abandon, from dainty florals and stripes to bold checks and plaids. It's a delightful balance of color and texture,

soft floral pinks with cool, soothing greens and rustic, rough-cut wood with smooth river stone. Its interiors are airy, uncluttered, and filled with natural light. They connect us to nature and open us to the landscape outside. Here, perhaps, is where the lush cottage garden comes into play, creating a welcoming transition to the outdoors and the kind of blissful alfresco living that today's modern cottage style celebrates. The best cottage gardens look quite accidental—a joyful, haphazard mingling of flowers, fruit trees, and fragrant herbs covering every square inch of land, encroaching on walkways, and climbing up trellises and exterior brick walls. Today's cottage gardens are unfussy and informal, taking on a decidedly natural look. Flowers are intentionally planted at the edges of garden beds and encouraged to spill over garden pathways. Arbors and trellises are essential for training vines,

roses, and other climbers to crawl upward above doorways, walls, and charming garden gates. Cozy benches and chairs delightfully tucked into the hidden enclaves of the garden beckon visitors to sit for a while and relish in the fragrant beauty.

Inside, each room is an inspiring composition of meaningful objects, well-curated personal collections, charming handmade crafts, and exquisite heirloom treasures. Furniture doesn't need to match, and pieces can range from the recycled to the rare. Period antiques can sit elegantly alongside flea market finds. Wood floors can easily be left bare or dressed sparingly with painted stencils or vintage rugs.

Regardless of location, cottage style is all about simplicity, comfort, and relaxed informality. But perhaps cottage style, above all, is a lifestyle—a blissful mindset that speaks from the heart and from the soul—the sincerest expression of home.

iselin | carruthers   beach stones   ▲ Abrams

iselin | carlson   seashells   ▲ Abrams

COTTAGES

Personal Stories of Hearth & Home

Cottage Revival

With a shared love for historic architecture, cottage gardens, and Colonial antiques, a design-savvy couple restored their 1909 waterside dwelling—Forsythe—to its former glory on Canada's majestic Lake Ontario.

Poised proudly on Olde Oakville's West Harbour, where Sixteen Mile Creek feeds into Lake Ontario, Forsythe gleams like the crown jewel of what was once considered "cottage country" for many affluent Torontonians. This stoic Georgian and Federal-style residence—originally clad in red clay brick, with a hipped roof and a traditional center hall plan—most certainly had great bones but was long overdue for a reinvention as well as some fresh, modern amenities. Luckily, Shirley and Ric Riordon, a Canadian couple whose passion for classic architecture equals their love for gardening, recognized the home's potential and quickly purchased the property. They immediately began an extensive three-year restoration that included not only the entire home but also the surrounding landscape.

"With the design of this property, we were aspiring to respect its history while introducing refreshing cottage lifestyle sensibilities," says Ric, founder of Riordon Design and The Fussy Gardener. "When working with an historic home, I believe the architectural style itself should inform the design approach," he notes.

To start, the couple revitalized the exteriors by painting over the red bricks in a soft gray-green hue called "Desert Twilight." A delectable cream shade—"Carrington Beige"—applied to the doors, windows, shutters, columns, and millwork provided an elegant contrast. To create the cottage-home feel they love, the Riordons replicated all the original trim detailing and enhanced the architectural character of their home with board-and-batten siding, plaster crown molding, coffered ceilings, wainscoting, recessed bulkheads, and beefy baseboards—all painted in Benjamin Moore's "Cloud White."

Completely restored, the dining area features a turn-of-the-century chandelier and a French parlor mirror that originally came from a grand home in upstate New York.

"Specifically, I'd say two driving influences for us are Colonial antiques and world travel experiences."

—RIC RIORDON

"The entrance seemed to lack importance," recalls Ric. "By borrowing inspiration from a 'bump-out' box bay detail on the side of the house, paneling the front door, and flanking it with bracket details and sconces, we solved this concern and also repeated this detail on the back entrance and garage for continuity," he adds.

Exceptional architectural details flow throughout the home and also work to create a seamless transition from the original structure to a new sunroom and master bedroom addition, and even to a freestanding carriage house-style garage. Weathered hickory floors in dark, rich tones provide a striking contrast to the couple's preferred interior palette of soft muted grays, pale blues, and warm whites—hues thoughtfully selected from an assortment of historic paint colors by Farrow & Ball and Benjamin Moore. A mixture of fabrics—sumptuous linens and cottons—resolve the tension between formal and casual. Slipcovered chairs and sofas, modern tables and accents, and a few select antiques from the Riordons' 40-year collection, helped define the cottage personality of Forsythe.

Small yet inviting, the living room features a striking antique glass-top table discovered at Sonoma Antiques in California.

"Specifically, I'd say two driving influences for us are Colonial antiques and world travel experiences," says Ric. "We love the unique, unmanufactured character of worn furniture pieces—one-of-a-kind treasures with a patina that only time and repeated use can create."

The Riordons' passion for both home and retreat—sanctuary and escape—motivate their impeccable design sense and extraordinary vision. For them, cottage style suggests a casual formality, a relaxed welcoming, a warmth and charm. Forsythe was an effort to design a space that personally expresses these attributes. Throughout their many travels, it has always been the special places by the sea—old town Grimaud overlooking the French Riviera; Ravello's Villa Cimbrone perched above Amalfi in Italy; Charleston, South Carolina; and Tenby, Wales—that align with this aesthetic and are undoubtedly the most memorable.

Working with the existing structure and the constraints of a compact space required being particularly thoughtful of space planning. The homeowners love the convenience of a galley kitchen where everything is within reach, enabling greater efficiency when preparing meals. Additional storage space nearby holds a large antique cabinet and built-in pantry cupboard for items not as frequently used.

The master bedroom was inspired by a visit to the Farmhouse Inn in Sonoma, California. "Painting this early 1800s bed took courage," says Ric. "The original wood had a beautiful patina but was too heavy for the look we were after."

"Both Shirley and I grew up in small historic towns on the Great Lakes," says Ric. "Olde Oakville, being near the water, creates that familiarity of home and holiday year-round for us, and the nearby harbor, marina, shops, parks, and walking trails along the lake make our home seem uniquely like a cottage in the city," he adds.

Relishing the surrounding scenery as well as their own well-designed gardens, the Riordons cherish Forsythe's new airy, lighthearted demeanor—especially the sunroom. The natural light and openness of the space lend a traditional modernity to their 100-year-old home. Surrounded by windows, it is their favorite place to relax and enjoy the blissful landscape outside.

"When I think of the most beautiful cottages and homes we've visited in Ireland, England, France, and Italy, the importance of a beautifully planned garden plays such a significant role in creating the overall impression," says Ric. "However complex or simple, the property and grounds define that experience of cottage for us. It's all about the views—the ones you control and the ones you borrow."

"Every cottage needs an antique hall clock," says Ric. "Just turn it off when there are guests who want to sleep."

Lowcountry Living

A marriage of coastal style with cottage coziness, this South Carolina retreat pays homage to its setting in one of the South's most scenic cities.

Bursting with culture, character, and centuries-old oaks, Bluffton is in the heart of the South Carolina Lowcountry. "It's the kind of place where kids run free, ride bikes around town, and enjoy the kind of blissful childhood we did," Krista Fowler, owner of Krista Fowler Interiors, says of the haven her Georgia-based family selected to build their vacation getaway. "When we're here, it's magical."

Krista and her husband, Cameron, were first introduced to Bluffton when they came to town for a destination wedding. The couple fell in love not only with the area's idyllic amenities, but also its majestic trees and Spanish moss. So, when they found a lot in the core of the Palmetto Bluff community's popular village, they decided to design with the area's lush live oak canopy in mind.

"We wanted a classic blue porch ceiling, but went with a twist and made it more of an aqua blue to bring in a little more modern feel that we then tied in to the shutters, too," Krista says.

The Fowlers selected architect Wayne Windham for his expertise with distinctive Lowcountry designs, and the result is a classic open-plan cottage that embraces its setting with pretty porches, great gathering spaces, and room for family and friends to settle in for a stay.

"We wanted guests to feel right at home, so each suite has a king bed, a private bathroom, and a color palette that feels fresh and relaxing," says Krista. "My aesthetic was a modern coastal farmhouse, so I blended old and new, feminine and masculine, and rustic and industrial."

In the master bathroom, Krista chose to play up the river setting with elements like driftwood-colored porcelain tiles and a pebbled shower floor. The downstairs powder room, accessible through a navy barn door, features mixed-material nautical touches, including a sand-like marble, reclaimed wood, a roped mirror, and an iron towel rod.

"Lighting is the accessory to every room.
Like wearing your favorite pair of earrings or
necklace, it does wonders to jazz up a space."

—KRISTA FOWLER

Reclaimed wood is carried through into the grand beams separating the family room and the dining area, where a focal point chandelier featuring May River oysters keeps the eyes up. The nautical farmhouse motif is then continued in these entertaining spaces via shiplap walls, a traditional table, a wooden beam mantel, an oyster shell tabby surround, and understated punches of blue.

The Fowlers knew their hardworking kitchen would need to accommodate a host of guests and feature indestructible surfaces, so the couple selected a zinc countertop for the kitchen bar and a sea pearl quartzite for the island and range countertops. Krista also chose to integrate some more modern elements, such as industrial stools and a chevron tile backsplash.

Of course, given its dreamy setting, the home's outdoor spaces pack as much appeal as the indoors. Off the master suite, a private porch provides a serene spot for a couple to enjoy morning coffee, and the screened porch off the kitchen features spa-like seating for everyone. "This is the kind of place that draws you out," Krista says. "Knowing the porches would become an extension of the indoors, we added ottomans, heaters, [and] even a swinging bed so that these spaces would be used year-round."

Nearly two years in, the home is serving as a sentimental spot not only for the Fowlers, but for their guests as well. "This home—this setting—is an incredible escape for our family, and it's a pleasure for others to get to share that, too."

With a fireplace, cozy heaters, a circular sofa, and view of the historic village green and the May River beyond, the screened porch off the kitchen is the heart of this Lowcountry home.

Fresh Starts

For these Nashville homeowners, the union of two families meant more than blending a set of parents and four children. It meant starting fresh in a home designed especially for them—one that married femininity and function in a timeless, family-friendly fashion.

"Classically built, this home's architecture steered away from trend," says designer Katie Gibson of Katie Gibson Interiors, "so we knew from the start that we wanted to reflect this style in the interior spaces." Her vision began with clean white walls—a blank canvas for traditionally lined furniture, unconventional fabrics, and plenty of pops of color. "The homeowner loves the look of French-Italian style, but she also leans toward a simple and feminine aesthetic," Katie explains. "So, rather than overdoing patterns, we focused more on interesting textures and intentional layering."

From the entryway, the home's symmetrical floor plan opens up to the dining and living rooms. On the left, the inviting dining area features a custom-made round table that seats the family altogether. The chairs are covered in a cheery fabric inspired by a large vintage mirror, one of Katie's early finds. Featuring seafoam and gold, the piece's palette also ties in a pair of console tables on the opposite wall.

Steps away, to the right of the foyer, the living room is anchored by a large Oushak rug. "With its gold, cream, and seafoam, this oversized rug was the perfect foundation for this room," Katie recalls. "We were able to then tie this pretty palette in through the layers of books, pottery, and art on the shelves." Another interesting accent includes the poppy tape trim at the base of the cream chairs, which entertained the client's passion for pink in a clever yet not too overwhelming way.

The designer selected this runner—a gift for her clients when the family moved in—as an easy element to pull the palettes of the dining and living rooms together.

"Rather than overdoing patterns, we focused more on interesting textures and intentional layering."

—KATIE GIBSON

"*I love the juxtaposition of traditional lines with these fresh, clean colors.*"

—KATIE GIBSON

Married in Naples, Florida, the homeowners have an affinity for the beach, an element the designer integrated through mother-of-pearl, shells, coral, and art. This particular painting even features the wife on a sandy stroll.

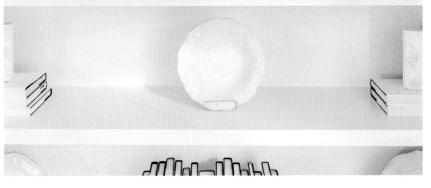

For the family's library, Katie complemented the rich wood with a soft purple and slate blue that would tie into the feminine colors of the rest of the house while keeping the library's distinctly cozy look. Layers of white accessories—including black-and-white family photos—help break up the heaviness of the built-in shelving while several sources of light—such as two lotus lamps with pleated shades—keep the space bright. Above the sofa, a commissioned marsh scene includes hues of soft peach, green, and blue.

Less is much more in this classic bedroom where elements like a gilded chandelier, soaring windows, monogrammed pillows, and a vaulted wainscot ceiling pack plenty of Southern style.

Perhaps the most neutral space in the home, the master suite is an airy retreat filled with whites, creams, and plenty of classic charm. Inspiration began with the exquisite bed, brought in from France and layered with soft ivory monogrammed linens. Not to detract from the focal point's elegance, the rest of the room's décor is understated, with trios of mirrors above the nightstands and a comfortable sitting area featuring a pair of traditional English armchairs and pale pink satin pillows.

"This is the kind of home that's easy to build off of," Katie promises. "Every room has fabulous light, gorgeous doors, great bones. Finding furnishings that would complement it was a joy—especially knowing that a new family would be making memories in it."

Seaside Serenity

A 1920s period replica bursts with character, nostalgia, and plenty of style.

I t was love at first sight—or first *stay*, to be sure—when Jacque Hamilton rented this chic bungalow-style retreat 14 years ago.

Just a short jaunt from the ocean in Florida's idyllic WaterColor community, the cottage was built as a historic replica of a 1920s California beach house. But what captivated Jacque most was its undeniably homey feel. "Beyond its cool vintage surf shack style, I couldn't forget its warmth, its coziness, and its supremely welcoming vibe," she recalls. "It reminded me of Grandma—in all the wonderful ways."

That first visit ended, years passed, and through a few twists of fate, in 2015, Jacque had the chance to make the home hers. "I couldn't believe my luck," she reveals, "and I've never loved owning a home more."

A beautiful blend of farmhouse and coastal cottage, "Buttercup"—affectionately dubbed after the name of its street—thrives on authenticity. From wood floors to planked boards, the nostalgia of the period home is reflected in its timeless design, purposeful color scheme, and carefully curated accessories.

Here, hospitality begins with the first step onto the home's broad front porch, which is encased with shutters that reveal sunlight, salty breezes, and the sounds of passersby. Visitors are encouraged to pull up a seat, with wicker armchairs, an ottoman, and a swinging daybed creating a cozy setting for mugs of morning coffee or glasses of evening wine.

Unexpected accents like antique-style rugs help make this exterior space feel like an extension of the cozy cottage's interior.

Inside, whitewashed wood planks line the walls from floor to ceiling, becoming a neutral canvas for the cottage's peppy palette. Indeed, Buttercup is a study of color, drawing inspiration from the sea, shore, and natural world, with pops of brick red, seafoam green, robin's egg blue, and sunny yellow, too.

Layered with pillows and throws, these plush slipcovered sofas and chairs are not only timeless, but also an easy-care option for high-traffic family rooms.

In the heart of the home, a timeworn farmhouse table is situated in the gourmet kitchen. Here, the whole gang can gather on vintage benches, allowing for family-style shrimp boils and late-night board games.

Rise and shine in this sunny bathroom where bright yellow trim and a classic claw-foot tub welcome guests to begin their day.

Up the staircase is the cottage's more whimsical suite, featuring built-in beds, a sitting area, and a duo of vintage-inspired sinks. "Kids love feeling like they have their own hangout up there; plus, it's packed with storage and an easy, breezy, quick-break-from-the-beach feel," Jacque says.

Walls of windows fill the cottage with natural light, which bounces off antiques and accessories that allude to the sea—driftwood, conch shells, sea grass, and more. Fishing poles, oars, tackle boxes, and license plates add to the Southern fish camp feel. Elsewhere in the home, elements like sumptuous bed quilts and slipcovered sofas can quickly transport Jacque into a vacation frame of mind. "Modern soft goods mix well with antique lighting and furnishings to show how a historic-style home can be both chic and authentic," she says.

Although this anything-but-typical suite most commonly appeals to younger guests, Jacque says everyone loves its "old-school California" appeal, including antique lighting and vintage sinks, plus sitting and dressing areas all splashed in bright shades of yellow and turquoise.

"Modern soft goods mix well with antique lighting and furnishings to show how a historic-style home can be both chic and authentic."

—JACQUE HAMILTON

These days, Jacque enjoys sharing her home with other Gulf Coast vacationers through her interior design and home rental company. But as she works to freshen the space, there's no doubt she's careful not to lose sight of what attracted her on that maiden visit. "This home has been such a blessing to my life. It's comfortable, it's serene, and it's most certainly familiar. I love sharing that feeling with others."

Hampton Bays

Tucked alongside old fishing ports and beautiful undeveloped beaches, this laidback Long Island cottage is the perfect weekend getaway for a creative city dweller.

Arguably just a short drive from downtown New York City, Richard Sinnott's laidback beach cottage seems light-years away from the frenetic pace of the city. Laden with vibrant colors, lively prints, and an ever-changing landscape of quirky collectibles, his comfy getaway set amidst Long Island's up-and-coming Hampton Bays offers an idyllic, let-your-hair-down escape from the refinement of his Manhattan apartment.

"Hampton Bays is an awesome little town with the most amazing undeveloped beaches and beautiful bays," says Richard, creative director for Michael Kors accessories. "I love the casual, unpretentious vibe—it's part of the Hamptons, but blue-collar Hamptons," he jokes.

A self-described "obsessive collector," Richard designed his 1930s cottage to be—among many things—warm and happy, fun to look at, bold, and brave. But most of all, he wanted it to be a curation of things that tell a story. He restored and "animated" all the architectural trims with integrity to their original style while taking an "anything goes" approach to the interior décor. Because this was going to be his weekend home, Richard felt he could really take risks and have fun, making this place feel distinctly different from the sleek restraint of his Gramercy Park abode.

OPPOSITE: "I love my foyer because it feels so roomy and open," says Richard. "The tramp art mirror came from a local New York City thrift shop, and the demilune table was a rare find from a Southampton antiques store," he notes. Richard plucked the bouquet of fresh hydrangeas from his own garden.

Made in the 1930s, the stone fireplace in Richard's beach cottage living room is embellished with semiprecious stones, including crystals, quartz, and turquoise. "I love this room," he says. "The fireplace is a work of art, and the handwoven rug is the most fantastic antique I've ever found." Preferring a hodgepodge of periods and styles, Richard pulls together disparate pieces—a folksy antique painting of a fox in the woods, an Art Deco mirrored table, a pair of elegant vintage Marbro lamps—with effortless panache.

"It was a blank canvas with so much to work with—the generous size, the gardens outside," he recalls. "I literally love *stuff*, and I love color and pattern—there is not much beige in this house, unless it's a coffee stain," he says with a laugh. "I love eclectic, too, so this home is my living space alter ego, with splashes of color everywhere, a mix of bold prints, and collected pieces I like regardless of period or style that just seem to find a place here," he says.

Filled with meaningful things that each tell a story, Richard's cottage holds an abundance of treasured pieces he's had since he was a boy and first started collecting. Among them, an extraordinary mantel clock and a turquoise beaded board kitchen cabinet both came from his parents' 1899 Victorian home. Other favorites in his well-curated cache include spectacular antique rugs, vintage café au lait bowls, and intriguing old paintings he's uncovered from thrift shops, off-the-beaten-path flea markets, and even an old van selling antiques off the main highway on the north fork of Long Island.

"If you open a cabinet, you won't find cereal," he quips. "You are more apt to find a vintage pottery collection, a group of 1930s head sculptures, or a box of ceramic hands," he says. "I have insane stacks of French bowls and at least 300 vintage linen tea towels. My go-to design tips for this place were basic: No rules. No worrying about what goes with this or that. I saw it, loved it, bought it, placed it. Done."

OPPOSITE: "I love all the open shelves in my kitchen, where I display my 1940s California dishware," says Richard. "I found the vintage Chambers oven on eBay, and I drove to Pennsylvania to pick up the vintage sink. The island was originally an antique dresser with a wood top, so I took it off and slapped on a slab of marble," he laughs.

Spending most of his time in the dining area of the kitchen, Richard cleverly put a sofa at the dining table—he had the legs raised to dining height—where he and his guests could relax and lounge for hours. The glass doors and windows looking out to the back garden let in amazing southern light, and the walls, painted in Benjamin Moore's "Straw," seem to glow all day long.

"I grew up with an Italian American mom, so the kitchen was the heart of our home," he recalls. "It's my hangout. I'm there every morning, and that's where my friends and I always sit," he says. "When I'm alone, I kick back on the pillows and just lie there and read."

Adjacent to the kitchen, Richard's dining room is his favorite hangout. "The curtains are made of vintage linen tea towels I had sewn and patched together," he notes. "I had piles of them in my cupboard, some with the original tags on them for like 9 cents," he says with a laugh. The sideboard is filled with Richard's favorite French café au lait bowls. "I got my first one in 1991 and have collected them ever since. I carried most of them back in my luggage from the many trips I took to the Paris flea markets," he says.

The oil and plaster paintings in the den were once part of a wall in a race car garage from the 1930s in Ohio. One of the mechanics was an artist and would paint the race cars on the wall of the garage. "I love them because they are naive and tell me a story," says Richard. "Old cars fascinate me—they have such style."

For the master bedroom, Richard mixed prints and color in serene shades of turquoise and coral. "Color calms me, especially blues and greens," he says. "The curtains were made from vintage Suzanis and the rug is an antique Serapi. The bed and brass-front antique chest were gifts from my very generous sister, Colleen," he notes.

A veritable scrapbook of his past and present tastes, Richard's cottage is forever evolving, along with his creative eye and spectacular style. Preferring a "my house is never done" approach, he finds it impossible to commit to a single look and humorously admits to having no patience for the streamlined sameness of Mid-Century Scandinavian.

"I can't sign up for just one period of style; it bores me," he says. "I like unique, found items—the hunt is the thrill—and I don't work with an interior designer, never have. They just don't know what I like, as I sometimes don't until I see it," he says. "All my choices come from my gut, my heart, my soul—I can't depend on anyone to understand that."

Seaside Chic

Nestled on the coast, this East Hampton cottage exudes classic style with a coastal twist.

Before you even step inside Susan and Mark Kendalls' summer home in East Hampton, New York, it's evident that the cottage has something special. The royal blue of the front door is a vibrant focal point for the front porch, and yet it's right at home amid the neutral tones that surround it. It's the first indication in the home that bold colors and strong prints—like the striped cushions on the vintage metal rope chairs—can come together with classic style choices to create a timeless, relaxing design.

The home is the work of New York-based interior designer Gregory Shano, who previously designed the Kendalls' New York City apartment with a "calm, subdued palette." Since the East Hampton home would mostly be used in the summer, the Kendalls gave him liberty to be bolder. "We wanted a bright, happy space that was stylish but kid-friendly," Susan says. "Greg inspired us to use more color and patterns in the design, and we are thrilled with the result. He struck a great balance between classic design and whimsical features."

That balance is seen throughout the home in bold patterns and bright colors that stand out against a background of neutral tones, natural woods, and linen fabrics. "When you work with strong colors like these—bright coral, aqua, and lime—you need to make sure there's a balance of neutrals present so it doesn't feel overwhelming," Greg says. "I wanted to have elements threaded throughout the house [that] gave a nod to the coastal surroundings without becoming too overtly nautical or gimmicky."

He incorporated those elements in places like the living room, where a sky blue sofa is flanked by rattan side tables and the bookshelf displays oversize shells and vintage seascapes. "They add such beautiful dimension to a room," Greg says of the paintings. "There's so much history behind them, and no two are alike."

Even in the art he chose for the home, Greg found a way to tie together timeless and modern styles. "There's a mix of new and vintage, which I always love," he says. He notes pieces like those in the living and dining areas, which help pull together the various shades of the color palette. "I try to identify the spaces that need a focal point and start from there," he adds.

In the kitchen, contemporary details defer to classic lines and natural wood. "With two young boys and an outdoor dining area and pool just off the back, this kitchen gets a lot of traffic, so we needed to make sure it felt light, clean, open, and user-friendly," Greg says. The wooden island, topped with quartz, features plenty of storage, and the white of the cabinets is echoed in the Emeco island stools.

Summery tones return in the dining room, where chairs by Restoration Hardware feature family-friendly faux leather in a cheerful green. The walnut dining table injects the space with a touch of timeless style, drawing out the natural tone of the textured rug below. "The dining room is located on the other side of the kitchen, and we wanted it to be suitable for when they're entertaining indoors, yet not feel overly formal," Greg says.

"We wanted a bright, happy space that was stylish but kid-friendly."

—SUSAN KENDALL

The home's coastal spirit spills onto the back deck, where navy-and-white throw pillows echo the combination of classic and contemporary found on the front porch. It's the final step toward Greg's goal for the design of the home. "I wanted to create a happy, comfortable home with loads of style that reflected the spirit and energy of their family," Greg says. "Seaside chic."

Vintage Charm
by the Sea

**This interior designer's home features subtle variations
on timeless style choices.**

When Greg Shano and Michael Giannelli purchased their
cottage in East Hampton, New York, it was a blank canvas.
"We purchased it from a couple who had just completed
a full renovation, so it was in pristine condition," Greg
says of the home, which was built in 1905. "All we did was re-stain the
floors in a dark ebony finish and paint the walls."

Owner of Gregory Shano Interiors, Greg set about creating a space that
reflected the tranquility of the surrounding area. "The goal was to create
a chic, relaxed summer retreat that had a classic, beachy Hampton vibe
to it," he says. "Since it's such a small house, I wanted to use a very calm,
neutral palette throughout the rooms to create a nice flow and keep the
eye moving, giving the impression of a larger space." Featuring beachy
blues and soft creams balanced by darker tones and bold prints, the home
is infused with a welcoming, vintage vibe.

In addition to the color palette, furniture choices were influenced by the home's smaller size. In the living room, Greg opted for a loveseat instead of a sofa and placed it in a bay window. "It makes that room feel so cozy and intimate," he says. He also found ways to be creative in the kitchen, where an island purchased from a restaurant supply company provides not only a place to eat but also room for storing dishware and other kitchen tools.

Much of the cottage's character comes from the vintage pieces that Greg incorporated into the design, which nod back to the home's history, saturating every space with a sense of days gone by. "I like punctuating the neutral palette with hits of the dark wood vintage pieces," he says. Most of the vintage and antique furniture found in the home—including dressers, armoires, and tables—were found at antiques shows and markets. "I wanted to mix in as many vintage pieces as possible," he notes.

"*The goal was to create a chic, relaxed summer retreat that had a classic, beachy Hampton vibe to it.*"

—GREG SHANO

Greg also incorporated vintage artwork, like the seascapes found in two of the home's three bedrooms. "I'm always fascinated by all the many different interpretations of them that exist, and I always find the colors so beautiful and soothing," he says. Bold navy-and-white-striped bedding contrasts with and complements the paintings, creating comfortable and inviting places to stay.

RIGHT: "The Flower Room," one of the two guest bedrooms in the home, features a pairing of airy blue bedding and still paintings rich with darker tones. The result is a space that would feel at home in any era. OPPOSITE: In the dining room, slipcovered cane back chairs are paired with a creamy white pedestal table. Weathered stone accents add a touch of character, and the ebony stain of the hardwood pulls the dark shades on the chandelier down into the space.

From the front of the house, the deck and pool area are accessed via a bluestone walkway featuring a vintage sundial. Boxwoods and hydrangeas surround the arched doorway leading to the back, creating a scene reminiscent of a storybook.

During the summer, the outdoor deck and dining area is a favorite spot for both relaxing and entertaining. While the interior of the home needed minimal work, Greg and Michael renovated the landscaping extensively. Now, the backyard is the perfect place to enjoy every balmy day that summer has to offer. "It's my favorite place to sit and relax," Greg says.

From front to back, this East Hampton cottage is brimming with timeless design. Through the use of neutral tones, vintage pieces, and creative furnishing choices, Greg infused the space with a calm aura, creating a time capsule of true cottage style.

Intentional Beauty

With a penchant for authentic architectural details, classic English gardens, and Colonial antiques, a Canadian couple designed and built the cottage of their dreams.

A labor of love both gratifying and exhausting, Forestwood was designed with all the beauty of Colonial classicism yet with all the convenience of modern amenities. Situated 30 minutes west of Toronto, just a short walk from the shores of sparkling Lake Ontario, the property is a vision, well planned and precisely executed by Shirley and Ric Riordon, a style-savvy couple who saw the project through to completion with impeccable forethought and patience.

"It was our dream to design and build a new house with all of the charm and character of a Colonial Georgian-style home," says Ric. "We were intentional about creating authentic details from the inside out while still providing the efficiencies of modern living. No detail was overlooked," he notes.

Nestled in a quaint cul-de-sac at the summit of a quiet street, Forestwood—the first of two of the Riordons' dream home renovations (see page 16)—meanders without sidewalks amidst pristine formal gardens and soaring mature trees, giving one the sense of being in the country. Taking inspiration from classic architecture and traditional English gardens, the property's exterior features include pilaster and dentil details, crown moldings, a gambrel roof extrusion off the main structure, Pennsylvania fieldstone chimneys topped with cedar shake roofing and copper finishes, Cape Cod prefinished clapboard, Marvin wood windows and doors, a side porch, and a gunite pool with herringbone brick and Wiarton stone paths. Inspired by traditional English gardens, a series of brick parterres, terraces, and pathways envelop and wind throughout this extraordinary property, along with more than 20 towering trees that frame the grounds and give prominence to this resplendent estate.

"Because we are such avid gardeners, the six English garden areas that surrounded Forestwood played an essential role in setting this property apart," says Ric. "By planting large-scale shrubs and trees to supplement the existing 26 established trees, the gardens looked remarkably mature in just three years," he adds.

The pool area and garden shed were designed by the couple to complement the architecture of the house. A pair of round antique windows were incorporated in the front and side gable. OPPOSITE: A custom wrought iron fence borders the pool area amidst the property's meticulously designed parterre and side gardens. Designed with herringbone Canton brick, Pennsylvania fieldstone, and comfy outdoor wicker furniture, the porch is the Riordons' favorite space.

Inside, classic architectural details and design enhance the nostalgic character of the couple's living spaces. Random-width plank wood floors custom-milled from a 150-year-old barn, refurbished antique mantels for three Rumford woodburning fireplaces, plaster moldings, and custom Colonial cabinetry, trim, and paneling details bring an element of authenticity and timelessness to Forestwood's airy and inviting interiors. Wonderful country-casual antique cupboards the couple has collected over the years serve both the aesthetic of the interiors and the practical need to store things. Many of these pieces still have their original finishes, bringing a beautifully rich patina and character to the space.

"Tongue-and-groove coffered ceilings, a fieldstone fireplace, slip-covered furniture, and antique accents really captured our vision for this room," says Ric.

A beautiful space to enjoy breakfast and entertain friends, the kitchen features custom cabinetry, granite and marble countertops, custom pendant lamps, and a veneer Canton brick wall behind the oven hood.

"I think less-formal antique pieces like these really enhance that sense of cottage and inform the style direction overall," says Ric. "We love the tension between stately formality and casual elegance, so we incorporated a blend of early Canadiana antiques, British 19th-century paintings, and relaxed furniture styles to adorn each room," he notes.

While the new house and surrounding grounds on page 16 are a bit larger, Forestwood was intentionally designed to feel human in scale and warmly inviting—never overtly grand or ostentatious. To better understand the lighting and the layout of the lot, Shirley and Ric actually lived in the original bungalow on the property before construction began.

"It took us two years to plan and build overall," Ric says, "and this particular home had so many unique areas we enjoyed both inside and out. Many of our neighbors would vacate for the summer to 'cottage country,' but for us, our home was our cottage, so we designed it with that aesthetic and ambience in mind," he adds.

Lavishly dressed in Ralph Lauren bedding, the guest room's refurbished 1800s Cannonball bed with its original finish steals the spotlight. OPPOSITE: Benny, the family's ginger Maine Coon, poses casually in the hallway alongside a balustrade replicated from an 1800s townhome.

The master bedroom provides a cozy retreat with paneled recessed windows, a circa 1800 canopy bed from Upper Canada, a Rumford fireplace, and an original oil painting by English artist Walter Williams.

Cozy in Cashiers

Featuring timeless, rustic style, this mountain cottage is a welcoming retreat tucked into a North Carolina canyon.

When Merrill Stewart found Lonesome Valley over five years ago, he knew that it was the perfect place to put down new roots with his family. The 800-acre community in Cashiers, North Carolina, is located among the Blue Ridge Mountains and features forest views and serene surroundings on land with a colorful history of mink and trout farming. The Stewarts began construction in August 2013. Now, their mountain abode is a inviting haven featuring warm tones, inviting spaces, and plenty of cozy corners for gathering with loved ones.

Before construction started, Merrill knew that he wanted to incorporate the home's surroundings into the design. "Prior to any grading of the property, we used a hydraulic crane to lift out the white pine trees from the site so as not to destroy the understory of mountain laurels and rhododendron below," he says. "We then took the trees to a mill nearby and had them sawed into rough-cut boards, then kiln-dried and milled into shiplap siding, which we used on the walls."

A metal arrow inlay, contrasted against the darker wooden surface, is one example of the attention to detail seen throughout the home.

The main areas of the cottage are connected by an open floor plan, allowing easy movement from the kitchen to the living and dining areas. Because the dining area opens onto the screened-in deck, it's easy to go from dinner with family to coffee by the fire.

The paneling features a light finish, which reflects the glow from the cottage's many windows and keeps the space feeling airy and relaxed. That relaxed tone is seen throughout the home in a color palette featuring creamy shades paired with natural materials like stone. White oak flooring from a nearby mill boasts a warmer finish than that of the walls, tying down the darker woods found in pieces like the dining room table. In places like the kitchen, pops of interest can be found in rich reds and deep blues, and decorative choices like land-scape paintings remind the inhabitants of the scene right outside the front door.

Bold contrasts are introduced in the kitchen, where a minimalistic island doubles as a breakfast table. The two-toned woven seats on the island stools tie in the darker shade of the kitchen cabinets, and the vibrant color choice on the window draws attention to the forest view outside.

The door to the ground-level den features a full prism of color in the form of door lites, which were crafted by an artist from Montevallo, Alabama.

Features of interest in the home's design include the wooden stairs that were crafted using a mortise and tenon joint, a method of construction that doesn't require the use of nails. Merrill also points out the history behind a number of material choices throughout the home, stating, "Our doors were made from the repurposed clear redwood of a 60-year-old water tank I found in upper Washington State." In addition, the hand-carved wooden mantel in the den bears spearheads that Merrill's father discovered in the Flint River near Albany, Georgia, in the 1930s.

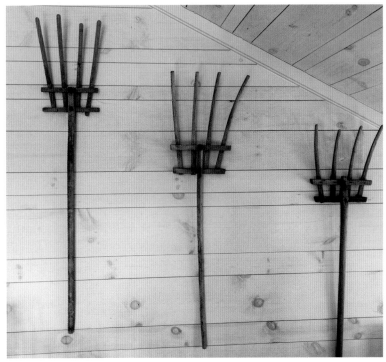

In every room of the home, the design is inspired and influenced by the mountain views that surround the structure on all sides. From the boats and paddles hanging from the ceiling to the baskets and idyllic folk art displayed on the walls, each design choice speaks to the quiet and serene lifestyle that is unique to mountain living. Every corner of the Stewarts' cottage offers a chance to relax, recharge, and reconnect with loved ones.

While many mountain homes are made heavy with an abundance of dark woods, the Stewarts' cottage welcomes in sunlight and fresh mountain air. Combined with the light finish of the wood paneling and the tans and beiges found on much of the furniture, it creates an effect that breathes tranquility into every room.

A Heart for Antiques

A history-loving couple finds their perfect century-old home on the West Coast.

Walking into the home of Diane and Jay Speakman is almost like entering a time capsule filled with charming trinkets from days of old. The shingled, white-trimmed East Coast-style home would be out of place in nearly any other town along the Pacific, but not in Gearhart, Oregon, where almost every house mimics that of the Speakmans. Just a few blocks from the center of town, it was the first in Gearhart Park, the predecessor to the now thriving community.

"My favorite room is the kitchen," Diane says. "We spend so much time there." Open shelving and a curtained and beaded board island add to the charm of the home.

Though situated on the Pacific Coast, the Speakmans' home has a classic New England style, with original shingled walls, white trim, and dormer windows. The ceiling of the couple's living room might look like a nice architectural detail, but it's actually the floorboards of the bedroom above.

The home, built in 1890, has remained almost the same. Over time, owners enclosed the porch that once wrapped around the entire house to add more living space. The Speakmans added a basement and steel beams for the foundation, but were firm in keeping the integrity and history of their home. "You know, a house kind of tells you what it wants," Diane says. "When you put a piece in a house, you just know what it asks for." And she speaks the language of her home perfectly, down to every piece. Turn-of-the-century antiques grace nearly every wall and vignette, in addition to paintings, china, transferware, and ironstone. "I'm a little obsessed," she admits. "I can't bring anymore in the house unless I take a piece out. I love antiques; that's where my heart is."

Diane integrates antiques not only into her décor, but into her furniture as well. "New furniture in this house just doesn't seem to go," she says. "I think I have an eclectic mix of a French and Swedish style, with Early American pieces mixed in." She incorporates rustic distressed paint details on the furniture with caning and French-style armchairs in nearly every room. She even went as far as to replace the simple fireplace that was original to the house with one she bought from a home just down the road that was built two decades later. The Speakmans cut no corners when it comes to using period pieces in their home.

Knob-and-tube wiring, standard electrical wiring from the late 19th century, is still visible in much of the house, including this upstairs bedroom. The Speakmans love the character and charm that it adds to the home. BELOW: A clean and bright color palette in addition to the window and French pitcher vase bring the outdoors into this bathroom.

In addition to maintaining the home's integrity through her furniture and décor, Diane has also made as few renovations as possible. You can still find knob-and-tube wiring in the master bedroom and upstairs hallway, and the original claw-foot bathtub is still in use. All the downstairs windows are single-paned, and the house is almost entirely single-walled and made from old-growth Douglas Fir. "The ceiling in our dining room is pretty high, but you're actually looking at the bottom of the floorboards of the bedroom upstairs," she explains.

In every detail, from the bare bones of the structure to the antique china hung on the walls, the Speakmans have let their house speak for itself. Over a century's worth of stories live within the walls, stories that radiate from the first step inside. In simply maintaining the integrity of their home, the Speakmans have preserved their own little piece of history along the Pacific Coast.

Nuance of New Orleans

A New Orleans designer thoughtfully and methodically restores her early 20th-century cottage bungalow with a fresh color palette and an eclectic mix of antiques and modern furnishings.

The raindrops tapping against huge banana leaves, the wind rustling through massive live oaks, the garden fountain bubbling amid the chatter of feeding birds, the nearby church bells pealing, the recognizable steel wheels from the historic New Orleans streetcar rolling slowly by just two blocks away . . . these are the soothing local sounds enjoyed from Emily Wright's front porch. An ambitious interior designer and proprietor of her own design firm, Emily purchased her early 20th-century cottage bungalow—along with its beloved porch—several years ago despite many levels of deferred maintenance and neglect.

"An apartment had been created by closing off the guest room area and adding a kitchen on the front porch," she says, laughing—and cringing—at the very thought of this decidedly unrefined renovation. "The new vision for this entire home restoration has been mine and has developed over many years as a fun and continuing labor of love," she says.

Built around 1908 in Moss Point, Mississippi, the home was relocated years later in three pieces by barge to its New Orleans setting. The original bones of the home—solid wood construction, expansive windows, high ceilings, original wood floors, a large enclosed front porch, and a corner lot with massive oak trees—were Emily's initial inspiration.

"I loved that, creatively, this house was a clean slate," the designer recalls. "It needed TLC from top to bottom, allowing me to execute my vision both inside and out," she says.

The large formal dining room has become a warm, inviting family room featuring custom-built bookshelves that were added around a bank of triple windows. The space now opens to a new dining area through an enlarged cased opening with a transom window inspired by the original doors of the home.

Doing so with the assistance of several critical collaborators, Emily was able to create a timeless, eclectic, and modern space while appreciating the intention of the original architecture. Belva Johnson, who was Emily's comrade in kitchen and bath designs over many years, helped to install a wet bar and copper farm sink to the newly refurbished front porch. Jeff Amann of Amann & Associates created an even better version of the front yard oasis than Emily had dreamed of by incorporating tropical plants, blooming perennials, azaleas, camellias, ginger, a Japanese maple that blooms in exactly the same color as the house, and the

creative placement of old Chicago bricks and salvaged iron fencing and gates from a demolished New Orleans home. The late Michele Lambert, Emily's dear friend and a local artist, hand stenciled and painted the new dining room floor, previously the back porch. Louis Aubert, a local colorist, provided expertise when selecting the exterior paint colors.

"I knew the deep 'Cottage Red ' hue was my choice for the body of the house," says Emily. "Louis expertly helped select the many accent colors that would pull it all together, providing the intensity and interest I wanted in a warm, subtle way," she notes.

"It needed TLC from top to bottom, allowing me to execute my vision both inside and out."

—EMILY WRIGHT

Emily's collection of late 19th- and early 20th-century family heirlooms works perfectly with the architectural style and age of her home. In her new dining area, a pie safe updated with green glass pulls now holds a china collection, and an old church pew and custom cypress dining table provide plenty of space for entertaining family and friends. An authentic, refurbished 1950s Chambers range anchors the kitchen, and an old wooden bed from Emily's great-grandmother washed with "Antique White" paint makes a charming focal point for the guest room. A restored antique gold Empire mirror and reupholstered daybed, both discovered in the French Quarter, nod to the French heritage of New Orleans while adding a bit of formality to the living room, along with a modern lantern chandelier and antique Turkish rug. A montage of drawings by New Orleans artist Philip Sage are displayed in the library, as well as a cherished poster of King Oliver, a famous local Creole bandleader and musician.

Turn-of-the-century cottages often included a butler's pantry that separated the kitchen from the dining area. Emily chose to remove her pantry and walls and replace them with custom upper and lower cabinetry and sleek copper countertops. Her new space offers a seamless, open view from the kitchen to the new dining area and converted family room and library. OPPOSITE: The custom-stenciled, hand-painted wood floor is the focal point of the tastefully appointed dining room that was once the original back porch. Double French doors and a crystal chandelier complement the antique church pew, the extended cypress dining table, and a pie safe that Emily transformed into a china cabinet.

Emily selected a whimsical combination of olive green and pink for the guest room. The striped fabric on the boudoir chairs combined with the olive green ceiling and bold draperies add a touch of warmth to the white bedding and walls.

"An eclectic mix of old and new is my favorite approach," says Emily. "I think it's important to reveal a homeowner's personal history—whether it's from travels abroad, inherited furnishings, a child's artwork, or a sentimental photo. Adding personalized touches makes the space feel authentic and unique," she notes.

Abiding by her own profession theme line—designing for the way you live—Emily was able to create a personalized space that truly reflects her tastes and her lifestyle.

"This is important," she says, "because once any design project is complete, a homeowner needs to love the outcome and feel like they're home—not just like they're visiting someone else's idea of their home," she adds.

Emily's covered screened porch offers a cozy outdoor living space to enjoy relaxing time with guests. Previously an awkward DIY apartment kitchen, her expansive porch was beautifully transformed with triple casement windows authentic to the original architectural style and double French doors with an overhead transom. Copper screening and a deep, copper farm sink and wet bar create the perfect outdoor dining space that also doubles as a gardening center.

WILLOW ST.

WELCOME

Undoubtedly, Emily's newly restored cottage bungalow feels like home, and the front porch is her favorite gathering space, with the kitchen running a close second. Come rain or shine, during any season, her guests always gravitate here. The covered, screened-in living and dining areas offer plenty of space for impromptu entertaining, and the lush front yard is the ideal spot for enjoying people-watching and all the familiar local sounds of New Orleans.

"The allure of my porch was beautifully expressed in a gift from my friends," says Emily. "It is a personalized sign by artist Simon [Hardeveld] of New Orleans that reads, 'What's Said On The Porch Stays On The Porch.'"

Nantucket Charm

This homeowner's request for a themed interior resulted in a Midwest vacation home brimming with New England appeal.

When one of Amy Studebaker's design clients requested a Lake of the Ozarks vacation home influenced by Nantucket, Massachusetts, she wasted no time in tackling the challenge. She traveled with one of the homeowners to the New England town, where they found no shortage of inspiration waiting for them. "When we were there, every home we went into, everything we viewed, all the stores, all the charm about this place was just so clean and soft and fresh," Amy says. "We wanted to bring that back into the home."

"*The home that we designed for them was really a lot about texture and interesting architectural elements.*"

—AMY STUDEBAKER

That influence is evident from the first moment you enter the Missouri home, which features a calm, clean color palette punctuated with the occasional burst of color. "The home that we designed for them was really a lot about texture and interesting architectural elements," Amy says. "And in my opinion, one way to keep those elements clean and fresh when you have so much going on is by keeping it white." In place of a wide range of hues, Amy chose to incorporate an abundance of texture. Shiplap, board-and-batten, linen window treatments, and weathered finishes add layers of interest to a home where vibrant tones are kept to a minimum.

Where color is used, it's used in a way that honors the home's surroundings. "We tried to pick greens and blues, which would remind us of the water," Amy says. Bold instances of these shades are found in places like the kitchen, where she chose to paint the island a deep green. "It gave the room some grounding and some depth while still keeping everything very light and refreshing," she says.

Crisp, airy linens and light woods in the bedroom fill the home with the serene essence of summer, and opening the French doors welcomes in balmy breezes from the lake. Throughout the home, strokes of vibrant color and bold accent pieces infuse every space with a spark of life.

Amy designed the study as a tranquil space for accomplishing tasks. "[The homeowners] can view the water just by looking up," she says. The only pop of color in the room is found in the aqua lamp, which stands out against the antique finish of the table and chair below. "Everything else is just very textural to keep it peaceful and soothing," Amy adds.

Outside, the clean color palette introduces darker tones than those found in the interior. Outdoor seating options feature deep navy cushions and throw pillows, offering a comfortable place to relax and enjoy the view.

Because the home sits on a peninsula, three of its four walls offer glimpses of the water outside, and the tranquility of the design helps draw attention to the view. "It's really about the use of windows and the placement of furniture to be able to look out the windows and take in the view outside," Amy says. "And then, again, keeping everything inside very simple and textural, so you can almost feel the outside being brought in."

Throughout the home, the design's inspiration also resulted in elements of classic cottage style.

"One thing that we picked up when we were in Nantucket was that there was so much charm in many of the homes," Amy says. "One thing that our client wanted to bring to this home was definitely some of that charm." Areas like the breakfast nook, which was designed with a step up, were created with the sole purpose of introducing cozy nooks and spaces to the home's interior. Despite its location not far from St. Louis, Missouri, the entire home is filled with Massachusetts charm and classic cottage style.

Minimal in Montana

Flathead Lake in northwestern Montana provides the perfect backdrop for a quaint cottage remodel for this busy pediatrician.

"They transformed my humble vision of a small cabin remodel into this dream of a sophisticated cottage," says homeowner Emily Hall. She can relax as her cottage renovation is now complete on Flathead Lake in Polson, Montana. "I often walk along the gravel roads with my dog, and on occasion, I'll canoe out to the surrounding islands for an exploratory hike."

Emily relocated to Flathead Lake from Seattle for a needed change. She began this project with a set of plans from another drafter and had been feeling that her vision of a "sophisticated cottage" was not being met. She then aligned with Angie Lipski and Sarah Ayers from MacArthur, Means & Wells Architects (MMW) in Missoula, and they re-worked her ideas into a functional space. "Already having invested money in the previous design process, Emily had a small amount left for our design," Angie explains. "We took her ideas and incorporated them, maximizing her design budget as well as trying to get her as much as possible for her limited construction budget." Emily's style is minimal, with monochromatic tones and simple, elegant furnishings.

The stairs to the second floor were the first thing to be moved because they pinched the living room into an awkward shape. Adding a 20x5-foot section to the front of the home enabled them to create a new entry and adjacent stairwell to the second floor, which opened up the living room and kitchen. Tackling the second story involved increasing the square footage by almost 300 feet. "Adding a dormer to the second floor created a wonderful master bedroom with beautiful views out to the lake," Angie notes. An unused room was converted to a reading room, and access to the attic is hidden in a secret passage behind the built-in shelving.

The living area is no longer pinched to an uncomfortable dimension by a stairwell, and now provides a cozy area for a beverage by the fire.

The windows in the kitchen face due-north, where Emily watches the changing weather on the lake and perfects her baking.

The MMW team was able to leave the existing plumbing in place, and moved the washer and dryer location from the basement into a closet stacked system off the foyer. The existing garage was also rebuilt, and Angie suggested that it be moved to the opposite side of the house in order to create a privacy barrier between her and her neighbors. Emily can access this new garage from the main house, allowing her to let her dog, Winston, out to run. The basement is accessed through a door below the deck, making it ideal for lake activity storage, which then frees up more space inside the home.

"For most, living near the lake is full of high-energy activities and recreational fun. For me," Emily says, "it's a place for reflection and solace. I spend most of my time after work in a hammock that hangs over the water in the shade of a tree." Emily looks forward to spending quiet time on the lake with Winston and plans to finish off the fence to her lot so that he has more space to run. "At no time did I think this remodel project would turn into my dream home, but now it's so perfect [that] I don't see myself ever moving," Emily says. "And as for Winston, he has not been on a leash since we left Seattle, and we both love it."

A quiet spot to read or to watch some television, this formerly unused room also provides access to the attic area behind a secret panel in the built-in shelves. OPPOSITE: Minimal décor and a soft palette lend to a calming atmosphere to enjoy the bedroom dormer's view of the lake.

A Sunshine State of Mind

Awash in ocean air and calming tones, this vacation cottage argues against the old adage that there's no place like home.

No matter where you're from, this rental home in Florida is the perfect place to get away for a while and still feel right at home. Amid clean lines and soothing colors, whispers of ocean breezes and tranquil seascapes pervade every inch of this beachside cottage.

The home belongs to Amy Johnson and her husband, who rent out the space when they are staying at their Georgia home. "I just wanted to add a little bit of color without making it dark," Amy says. "I wanted to keep everything open and bright." That goal is reflected in areas like the living room, where boldly patterned pillows lend sparks of color to more neutral slipcovers.

Rather than using the loud prints and typical beach imagery found in some Florida vacation homes, Amy said that she wanted "something very clean and modern." Even in the color choice for the curtains, she opted for a powder blue that adds a hint of color while maintaining the room's airy feel.

Cool gray island stools are the perfect place to grab lunch after a dip in the pool, and they add a subtle stroke of color to the white space. Metal mesh light shades above the island contribute a touch of industrial style, and minimal upper-level cabinetry allows for an abundance of sunlight. For dashes of color, designer Libby Baker Speight of Baker Design Company relied on a sky blue decorative plate hung from the backsplash and ocean-inspired wall art.

Since Amy and her husband love entertaining, a large dining space was a must. A rustic farm table provides plenty of room to gather, and cushioned wicker chairs add texture along with an extra layer of comfort. But Amy also saw a need to let everyone have their own place to retreat to and relax. "I just kind of wanted to create a lot of space where everybody could do their own thing or come together in a big open area," she says.

Cozy spots like an armchair next to the stairs are perfect for curling up and enjoying a light read on days when the weather isn't beach-friendly. Drops of color in the form of paisley-inspired pillows rest next to an aqua throw that's handy on cooler summer mornings.

In the guest room, darker shades like navy come into the mix while the white ceiling and trim keep things from becoming too heavy. A windowed nightstand displays books and other items, and the thin-striped area rug adds interest without detracting from the bold prints on the bedding.

On the third level, the children's bedroom provides kids with their own space. A modern-looking table with matching chairs offers a spot to play games or just spend time together, and built-in bunk beds feature reading lights and plush pillows, making them the perfect place for staying up or sleeping in. No matter where the young traveler is from, a miniature globe on the nightstand is a subtle reminder of home—and of all the trips yet to be taken.

"I just wanted to add a little bit of color without making it dark. I wanted to keep everything open and bright."

—AMY JOHNSON

GARDENS

Inspired Natural Landscapes

California-Style Garden

Floral designer Margaret Lloyd creates an exuberant landscape that thrives in a thirsty climate.

Although Margaret Lloyd's garden is in drought-stressed Santa Barbara County, California, it looks as luxuriant as an old-fashioned English cottage garden. Her secret? A lavish abundance of succulents and drought-tolerant natives as well as exotics that Margaret has combined with the eye of an artist.

She began creating the garden five years ago when she and her husband downsized to a two-bedroom house in an old, established neighborhood. They built retaining walls at the back and front of the property and brought in truckloads of rich soil to level the slopes and improve the native clay. To create more space for outdoor living, they expanded the original small backyard patio and built a large fireplace in one corner. "We entertain a lot," says Margaret, "so we need yard space."

Within the modest dimensions of the grounds—20 feet in front and 30 feet in back—Margaret laid out meandering paths and, as she puts it, "little rooms where people could gather and talk." Originally, she planted eight rose bushes in the backyard to use in her floral designs and wedding work. "The gophers ate seven of them," she says, "so I put pots of succulents in that spot." In the front yard, sheltered by the walls of the courtyard and house, 15 rose bushes and a variety of dahlias have so far eluded the hungry pests.

The rest of the garden is a tapestry of plants that can survive with little water. The previous owners of the home had planted agaves. When the Lloyds began reworking the landscape, Margaret dug them up and potted them until she could replant in the new beds.

Since then, she has added between 25 and 50 varieties of succulents, most given to her by neighbors and friends. "Succulents are something we can give each other because the cuttings root so easily," she says. "I use a lot of little succulents I clip in corsages and bouquets. They are so resilient, you can pull them off the bouquet and plant them and they will root. It's a nice keepsake from the wedding flowers."

Some of Margaret's favorite roses are the highly fragrant, peony-like 'Yves Piaget' hybrid teas and the 'Koko Loko' floribundas, which boast an unusual, subtle hue that blends latte and lavender.

"*If you go hiking in the local hills and see what's growing naturally, you can make growing a lush garden happen.*" —MARGARET LLOYD

Large agaves and burgundy-and-green aeoniums anchor the path that winds through the property.

Hardy natives, such as salvia and alyssum, and imports from South Africa and Australia complement the succulents. Margaret also plants for fragrance. "The tall salvia along the walk has a wonderful scent," she says. Roses, mint, California bay, lavender, honeysuckle, and jasmine also provide scented accents for her wedding work—and her own enjoyment at home. "My youngest daughter, when she comes for a visit, always expects lavender on the bedside table," she says.

Margaret's garden is both a personal passion and a resource. In her boutique business, Margaret Joan Florals, she specializes in wedding and event flowers, using what she grows to give her work a distinctively California look. Depending on what the bride wants, Margaret can supply up to 75 percent of the material for a bouquet from her garden. When she must buy flowers, she relies as much as possible on local and American growers to support the Slow Flowers movement. This four-year-old effort by the American floral industry encourages the use of locally grown flowers, which means relying heavily on what is seasonally available.

In spite of the very un-English climate of Montecito, California, Margaret has succeeded in creating a garden that evokes the cottage style. "If you go hiking in the local hills and see what's growing naturally," she says, "you can make that happen. We don't live in a desert; there's just not much water. But things grow."

Stewarding a Legacy

When Betsy Mills inherited the garden with deep roots surrounding a summer cottage in Maine, she was ready to dig in and bring it to the next level for another generation.

Visit Betsy and Quinn Mills's garden in Bar Harbor, Maine, and you immediately sense its pedigree. Penetrate into the depths of these deep borders, and it becomes readily apparent that this garden is the work of genius. Carefully configured, seamlessly balanced, and color-canny, perennials with a past waltz through the garden at the Farm House. With the garden faithfully restored to reflect its heyday, the insight and expertise of famed landscape architect Beatrix Farrand is evident every step of the way. But still, the garden shows very current understandings and eco-conscious sensibilities.

Cunningly, Farrand opted to install an interior-style staircase to access the house from the driveway. "It is a wonderful surprise entrance rather than the usual stone steps," says Betsy.

Farrand was a groundbreaker in her time. The niece of renowned novelist Edith Wharton, Farrand drew from the privilege of a New York City high society upbringing combined with an education at Harvard University's Arnold Arboretum and became a founding member of the American Society of Landscape Architects (in fact, the only female founding member of that organization). In 1928, Farrand was engaged by Miss Mildred Day McCormick to convert the gardens at the Farm House from their former food-producing focus (they supplied produce for the family's nearby summer mansion) to a more flowery function. Farrand laid out a neat network of voluptuous flower beds dense with perennials in soft pastels behind the "dollhouse" of a summer cottage. That garden was the delight of Miss Mildred who added wings to the quaint house and furnished the garden in fitting ornaments. She made constant use of the plants that filled her borders, snipping flowers for bouquets to decorate the house. But toward the end of her long life, when her eyesight began failing, Miss Mildred gave maintenance over to a local nursery who ripped up the carefully selected perennials and installed annuals instead. When Betsy inherited the property in 1981, the garden was certainly not in ruins, but it was only a shadow of its former self.

Betsy prepared for her new role by studying at Radcliffe and Harvard School of Design. When the time came to take the Farm House under her wing, she swung into action with a purpose, obtaining the original plans for the 80-foot borders from Farrand's archives at Berkeley. The plans were intricately detailed with specific perennials mapped out. Unfortunately, many of the original plants were no longer in popular cultivation. The tide turned when Betsy noticed some perennials sprouting from the compost pile and discovered a trove of original plants that had been tossed out. She sent them to be identified by Gary Koller, her instructor at Radcliffe. Thanks to his encyclopedic botanical knowledge, she was on her way to restoring the height, texture, and hues of the garden as they were originally designed.

The armillary sundial surrounded by everblooming roses and Asiatic lilies accents the axis looking over to the pergola where the Mills family enjoys breakfast, lunch, and drinks.

"It's a garden of secreted spaces. The arbor is like a window you look through to the excitement of the next destination."

—BETSY MILLS

Aristolochia (Dutchman's pipe), Virginia creeper, and sweet autumn clematis clamber over the pergola. A border of ferns, Actaea, and meadowsweet runs alongside.

But this is not a time capsule. Gardens evolve, and a wise gardener rolls with the punches. Betsy's first move was to trim the surrounding trees, allowing light to penetrate into the arborvitae hedge that surrounds the garden. She widened pathways, added borders, and installed a pergola based on the design of a similar nearby garden structure by Farrand. She flavored her garden with new understandings—adding and preserving native shrubs with an emphasis on coastal-adapted varieties, increasing the orchard with mature trees salvaged from a mainland orchard when it was about to be destroyed, and underplanting the apples with a meadow crisscrossed by mown paths. As a result of all the care and concern lavished on a scene that could easily have slipped into oblivion, the garden is again proud and promises to shine into the future.

By midsummer, the garden is a mass of blossoms with Echinops, Physostegia (false dragon head), phlox, stachyses, and daylilies all performing simultaneously. OPPOSITE: The double hollyhock 'Peaches and Dreams' shoots up so tall that the gardener must mount a ladder when staking against the coastal Maine winds.

Formality with a View

By framing open land against classical lines, fields become a garden and a landscape of many destinations takes shape. It's all part of living in the land.

The pineapple gate is always open to Debbie and Tom Meek's backyard. In addition to a warm welcome, the "open gate policy" is also a coaxing gesture luring everyone to slip behind the house and partake of the panoramic view. But Debbie and Tom's Connecticut landscape does not halt at the gardens immediately around the house. Instead, your glance is enticed outward to become mesmerized by the fields and ponds stretching into the distance. The beauty of this collaboration between meadow and man is the classical framework. By setting the natural landscape against formal borders, house and beyond both sing.

When Debbie and Tom found the Connecticut cottage, it was well on its way to spectacular. The previous owner was an antiques dealer who added several astute accessories to the house. He installed the ornamental fence and gate that obscure the backyard and its stupendous view for a magnificent *ta-da!* revelation. With a wise nod toward whimsy, he also inserted the first clipped poodle-cut boxwood topiaries that stand sentinel to frame the view. And he planted the low boxwood hedge that smartly finishes the bumped-out perennial beds embracing the back terrace. The espaliered fruit trees joining limbs to waltz along the side of the house are his insightful addition. In fact, in 2010, when Debbie and Tom arrived with a realtor to see the property (the last stop in a long property-shopping spree), the package was beguilingly irresistible. "We just loved everything—especially the extra touches," says Debbie. They fell for the 10-acre property before even entering the house.

The barn/bungalow also serves as a pool house surrounded by a safety fence softened by shrubs. For continuity, a cupola echoes the crown topping the main house.

Pruned boxwoods and shaped rhododendrons ground the front of the house while serving as a strong foundation, but the cupola gives the configuration flair. OPPOSITE: Fittingly painted red, the guest barn has large picture windows looking out to view the salvias and cosmos of the sundial garden.

Debbie was nervous. Intimidated by the level of care the property had been receiving, she worried, "Could I maintain the property in the manner to which it was accustomed?" But commitment and good taste came to her rescue. Plus, she hired Deirdra Wallins, a savvy local garden designer who helped with everything from plant choices to overall planning. In the end, not only did the Meeks sustain the integrity of their landscape, but they also added further flourishes and gardens. Most importantly, every move respects the land.

Both classical and whimsical, espaliered apple trees link limbs along the west side of the house, setting the mood for the entire property. Boxwood orbs run along the ankles of the fruit trees, bedded in dianthus and thyme.

The comfy furniture on the back terrace serves like a living room to coax the family out at the end of the day. Debbie plants containers and sends her houseplants outdoors for a fresh summer air vacation.

The Meeks are drawn outdoors, and their outward-bound lifestyle is reflected in the gardens that were renovated and added under their watch. The back terrace is their most frequent go-to lounging area, where they take drinks and watch the entertainment of birds, dragonflies, butterflies, and other wildlife happening in the meadow. For supper, they dine at a candlelit table on the terrace and then sink into Adirondack chairs by a dock and beach built beside one of the ponds for dessert. Later, after meandering the network of paths that Tom created in the meadow of goldenrod, mountain mint, Queen Anne's lace, bachelor's button, ironweed, and milkweed, they can enjoy a home away from home on their own property by settling down

beside the barn/guest bungalow. Situated on the far side of a foot bridge, the guest barn became a regular destination when they expanded the garden to create a world all its own.

Debbie calls her style "formal with funk." And as she worked with her land, her bond became stronger and she achieved an easy rapport with the gardens. Now, maintenance is a breeze as she shoulders more responsibility and tackles new projects. But the essence of the land remains the same. Slip through the gate of this Connecticut landscape today, tomorrow, or in a few years and the panorama will be there to greet you. Nature is preserved and elevated with a little formal framework and some help from its friends.

The craftsman-quality pineapple gate opening out to the back terrace and view is always ajar. Clipped boxwoods and beautifully selected lanterns add to the formality. OPPOSITE: Ginger the rescued golden retriever mix finds a shady spot to bask beside poodle-cut topiary boxwoods framing the view from the back terrace.

CREDITS

Cover by Donna Griffith

Cottage Revival
Pages 16–31

Photography by Donna Griffith. Text by Jeanne Delathouder. Designs by Ric Riordon of Riordon Design, 905-339-0750 or *riordondesign.com*. Landscape design by Ric Riordon of The Fussy Gardener, 416-802-4582 or *fussygardener.com*. Architectural design by Hicks Design Studio, 905-339-1212 or *hicksdesignstudio.ca*.

Lowcountry Living
Pages 32–45

Photography by Atlantic Archives, Inc./Richard Leo Johnson. Text by Lauren Eberle. Architectural design by Wayne Windham of Wayne Windham Architect, 843-815-3266 or *waynewindhamarchitect.com*.

Fresh Starts
Pages 46–59

Photography by Alyssa Rosenheck. Text by Lauren Eberle. Interior designs by Katie Gibson of Katie Gibson Interiors, *katiegibsoninteriors.com*.

Seaside Serenity
Pages 60–75

Photography by Colleen Duffley. Text by Lauren Eberle. For more information on the Buttercup Cottage, go online to Exclusive 30A, *exclusive30a.com/rentals/41* or call 844-STAY-30A.

Hampton Bays
Pages 76–89

Photography by Tria Giovan. Text by Jeanne Delathouder. Antiques by James McGuire Antiques, 631-723-3928 or *facebook.com/jamesmaguireantiques*, and Doyle, 212-427-2730 or *doyle.com*.

Seaside Chic
Pages 90–97

Photography by Tria Giovan. Text by Bethany Adams. Interior designs by Gregory Shano of Gregory Shano Interiors, 917-399-4334 or *gregoryshano.com*. Exterior landscaping by Whitmores Landscaping, Inc., 631-267-3756 or *whitmoresinc.com*.

Vintage Charm by the Sea
Pages 98–105

Photography by Tria Giovan. Text by Bethany Adams. Interior designs by Gregory Shano of Gregory Shano Interiors, 917-399-4334 or *gregoryshano.com*. Exterior landscaping by Dellapolla Landscaping, 631-267-2491 or *dellapolla.com*.

Intentional Beauty
Pages 106–119

Photography by Donna Griffith. Text by Jeanne Delathouder. Designs by Ric Riordon of Riordon Design, 905-339-0750 or *riordondesign.com*. Landscape design by Ric Riordon of The Fussy Gardener, *fussygardener.com*. Architectural design by Hicks Design Studio, 905-339-1212 or *hicksdesignstudio.ca*.

Cozy in Cashiers
Pages 120–135

Photography by Don Breland. Text by Bethany Adams. Built by Jennings Custom Homes, 828-743-2307 or *jenningscustomhomes.com*. Interior architectural design by Michael O'Kelley, 205-238-9334 or *okelleyarchitecture.com*.

A Heart for Antiques
Pages 136–145

Photography by John Ellis. Text by Hannah Jones. Styling by Sunday Hendrickson. Interior design by Sesame and Lilies, 503-436-2027 or *sesameandlilies.com*.

Nuance of New Orleans
Pages 146–157

Photography by Mac Jamieson. Text by Jeanne Delathouder. Interior designs by Emily Wright of Emily Wright Designs, 504-382-4439 or *emily@emilywrightdesigns.com*. Kitchen and bath designs by Belva Johnson, 504-443-1467. Landscape design by Jeff Amann of Amann & Associates, 504-862-9177.

Nantucket Charm
Pages 158–167

Photography by Alise O'Brien. Text by Bethany Adams. Interior designs by Amy Studebaker of Amy Studebaker Design, 314-440-0853 or *amystudebakerdesign.com*.

Minimal in Montana
Pages 168–175

Photography and text by Jeff McLain. Architectural designs by Angie Lipski and Sarah Ayers of MacArthur, Means & Wells Architects, 406-543-5800 or *mmwarchitects.com*.

A Sunshine State of Mind
Pages 176–181

Photography by Colleen Duffley. Text by Bethany Adams. Built by Jason Romair of Romair Construction, Inc., 850-654-3023 or *romairhomes.com*. Architectural design by Steve Dungan, 850-267-0053 or *designs@dunganarchitecture.com*. Interior designs by Libby Baker Speight of Baker Design Company, 850-972-9193 or *bakerdesignco.com*. Vacation rental management by Cottage Rental Agency, *cottagerentalagency.com*.

California-Style Garden
Pages 184–195

Photography by Emily Reiter/Anna Delores Photography and Rhianna Mercier. Text by Vicki L. Ingham. Floral design by Margaret Joan Florals, 805-705-8884 or *margaretjoanflorals.com*.

Stewarding a Legacy
Pages 196–205

Photography by Kindra Clineff. Text by Tovah Martin. Landscape design by Elizabeth Mills Landscape, *elizabethhmills@gmail.com*.

Formality with a View
Pages 206–217

Photography by Kindra Clineff. Text by Tovah Martin. Garden design by Deirdra Wallin, *deirdrathepersonalgardener@gmail.com*.